For all the military children.

To my beautiful Elena, my inspiration

My daddy is in the Navy!

He protects

our country.

He works on submarines.

Submarines are boats that go under the water.

Its fun

visiting Daddy

on the

submarine.

Sometimes Daddy leaves for a short time.

And sometimes Daddy leaves for a long time.

I miss Daddy when he leaves.

And my kisses will reach all the way to Daddy.

Sometimes we can send packages to Daddy.

We send him pictures we made for him.

When Daddy ports he can call us.

My Daddy has traveled all over the world.

Sometimes he gets me presents from other countries.

It's okay to miss Daddy and be sad.

Underways and deployments don't last forever.

Made in the USA
Coppell, TX
02 September 2021